12 WOMEN IN ENTERTAINMENT

by Marne Ventura

12 STORY LIBRARY
MORE TO EXPLORE

www.12StoryLibrary.com

12-Story Library is an imprint of Bookstaves.

Photographs ©: Kathy Hutchins/Shutterstock.com, cover, 1; Kathy Hutchins/Shutterstock.com, 4; Sk Hasan Ali/Shutterstock.com, 5; Globe Photos/ZUMAPRESS.com/Alamy, 6; sundawncer/PD, 7; Joel Ryan/Associated Press, 8; UNHCR HK/YouTube, 9; Asylum Records/PD, 10; Paul C Babin/PD, 11; PD, 11; vipflash/Shutterstock.com, 12; Pedro Mendoza/Associated Press, 13; kate gabrielle/CC2.0, 14; Robert Sullivan/PD, 15; PD, 15; Tinseltown/Shutterstock.com, 16; Gage Skidmore/CC2.0, 17; Brett Oronzio/Walt Disney Television/CC2.0, 18; Mark Humphrey/Associated Press, 19; Associated Press, 20; Kobby Dagan/Shutterstock.com, 21; Everett Collection/Shutterstock.com, 22; Pete Souza/PD, 23; William P. Gottlieb/Library of Congress, 24; William P. Gottlieb/Library of Congress, 25; Ron Adar/Shutterstock.com, 26; David Shankbone/CC3.0, 27; Robert Fulton/Library of Congress, 27; usbotschaftberlin/PD, 28; Kathy Hutchins/Shutterstock.com, 29

ISBN
9781632357762 (hardcover)
9781632358851 (paperback)
9781645820567 (ebook)

Library of Congress Control Number: 2019938624

Printed in the United States of America
September 2019

About the Cover
Priyanka Chopra in 2019.

Access free, up-to-date content on this topic plus a full digital version of this book. Scan the QR code on page 31 or use your school's login at 12StoryLibrary.com.

Table of Contents

1

Priyanka Chopra: From Bollywood to Hollywood

Priyanka Chopra is an Indian actress, film producer, and philanthropist. She was born in 1982 in India. Her parents were doctors in the Indian Army. In 2000, she won the Miss World pageant. She planned to go to college. But she was offered a job in an Indian film.

She became a big Bollywood star. Bollywood is the name for India's film industry. Chopra was praised for her beauty and her skill as an actress. She starred in many films. In 2008, she starred in a film called *Fashion*. She won many awards for this role. It was one of the first films in India with a female main character. Chopra became one of the highest-paid actresses in India.

Priyanka Chopra on a summer press tour.

In 2015, the American TV show *Quantico* came out. Chopra was the main character. This was the first time a South Asian was chosen to star in an American TV series. In 2017, she starred in the movie *Baywatch* with Dwayne "The Rock" Johnson and Zac Efron. She has a reputation for playing strong, confident women.

Chopra at a UNICEF press conference in 2018 after her visit to Rohingya refugee camps in Myanmar.

Chopra started the Priyanka Chopra Foundation for Health and Education. She gives 10 percent of the money she earns. The foundation helps needy children in India. It pays for education and health care. Chopra also speaks out on women's rights. She calls for equal jobs and pay for women in India. She works with UNICEF to promote children's rights. She started a film company in India called Purple Pebble Pictures. Its mission is to help talented Indians who want to work in the film industry.

50+

Number of movies Priyanka Chopra has acted in

- Chopra was the first Indian actress to win a People's Choice Award.
- She married Nick Jonas, one of the Jonas Brothers, in 2018.
- In 2019, she launched her own YouTube series.

2

Aretha Franklin: Queen of Soul

Aretha Franklin circa 1960.

A singer, songwriter, and activist, Aretha Franklin was known as the Queen of Soul. Born in Tennessee in 1942, she grew up in Detroit, Michigan. Her father was a well-known preacher. When she was 10, Franklin began singing at her father's church. She went with him on church tours. He gave sermons and she sang gospel songs. Franklin and her father worked with civil rights activist Dr. Martin Luther King Jr. Franklin recorded her first gospel music album when she was only 14 years old.

75,000,000+

Number of records Aretha Franklin sold in her lifetime

- Franklin won 18 Grammy awards.
- She also won the National Medal of Arts and the Presidential Medal of Freedom.
- She performed at the inaugurations of presidents Jimmy Carter, Bill Clinton, and Barack Obama.

Franklin was 18 when she began recording songs for mainstream record companies. She sang jazz and blues. By 32, she had made the Rhythm and Blues Top 10 list 33 times. Her songs were played often on radio stations that had not played music by black artists before. She was good at many different kinds of music. She even sang opera at the Grammys in 1998.

Franklin was active in the civil rights and women's rights movements. Her songs "Respect" and "(You Make Me Feel Like a) Natural Woman" became anthems for activists' groups. She donated money to civil rights groups and performed at their benefits and protests.

THE ROCK & ROLL HALL OF FAME

The Rock & Roll Hall of Fame is in Cleveland, Ohio. It was founded in 1983. Its mission is to recognize and record the history of the best rock and roll artists. In 1987, Aretha Franklin became the first woman to be inducted into the Rock Hall. Since then, 55 more women have been inducted, and 32 are black women.

3

Yao Chen: China's First UN Goodwill Ambassador

Yao Chen is a Chinese actress, activist, and social media superstar. She was born in 1979. Her father was a train driver. Her mother was a postal worker. She studied at the Beijing Film Academy. Her first role was in a martial arts sitcom. She went on to star in romantic comedies. She also made action films. Chen's shows and movies were very popular.

When she became successful, Chen began to work for refugees. She is China's first Goodwill Ambassador for the United Nations High Commissioner for Refugees. She travels to countries such as Ethiopia and Lebanon. She meets with refugees. She tells others about the refugees' needs. Journalists write about her visits, and more people learn about the plight of refugees. Chen also uses social media. She writes about her visits on Weibo, a Chinese website. Weibo is like Twitter. Chen has more Weibo followers than there are people in Britain.

Donations from China to the UNHCR tripled between 2012 and 2013. The UN believes this is due in part

Yao Chen in 2016.

Chen (right) visits with refugee families to learn about their needs.

to Chen's work. Chen also writes on Weibo about social issues in China. She calls for free speech and clean air.

ABOUT THE UNHCR

A person who must leave home because of war or persecution is a refugee. Two-thirds of refugees today come from Syria, Afghanistan, South Sudan, Myanmar, and Somalia. The United Nations High Commissioner for Refugees (UNHCR) helps refugees find new homes. It helps them stay safe and healthy and get education.

80,570,259

Number of Yao Chen's Weibo followers in 2017

- Chen has made the Chinese-speaking world more aware of refugees.
- In 2014, *Forbes* magazine ranked her the 83rd most powerful woman in media and entertainment.
- She is called "China's answer to Angelina Jolie." Jolie is an American actress who also works for refugees.

4

Joni Mitchell: Staying True to Herself

Joni Mitchell is a Canadian singer-songwriter. She was born Roberta Joan Anderson in 1943. Her parents lived in a small, run-down house. It snowed a lot. She was often sick. At age nine, she came down with polio. She had to stay in a nearby hospital for several months. Her left hand was damaged from the disease. Later, she invented new ways to tune and play a guitar because of this injury.

Mitchell loved music and art, especially painting. She went to college to study art. In 1964, she left school and moved to Toronto. She sang and played piano and guitar at coffeehouses. She married a folk singer. In 1967, she moved to New York City. She recorded her first album. People liked her lyrics. They told about her life. She was not afraid to sing about her fears and guilt as well as her joy. She was very open about her feelings.

Joni Mitchell in the 1970s.

Mitchell kept writing and recording songs. She released new albums almost every year into the 1980s.

THINK ABOUT IT

Many music critics admire Joni Mitchell. One reason is her willingness to try new things. For example, she tuned her guitar in a new way. Was this risky? Why or why not?

Mitchell in concert in 1974.

She was known for experimenting with different genres. She worked in folk, pop, rock, folk-rock, and jazz. She didn't worry about whether her music would be popular. She followed her own interests and tried new things. Mitchell never stopped painting. She painted the covers for almost all of her record albums.

8

Number of Grammy awards Joni Mitchell has won

- Mitchell was inducted into the Canadian Music Hall of Fame in 1981.
- In 1997, she was inducted into the Rock & Roll Hall of Fame.
- She received a Grammy Lifetime Achievement Award in 2002.

5

Shakira: Helping Thousands of Children

Shakira on the red carpet.

30,000

Number of people in Colombia who are helped by Shakira's schools

- 6,000 students go to Pies Descalzos Foundation schools.
- Shakira is an advocate for early childhood development.
- She served on President Barack Obama's Educational Excellence for Hispanics commission in 2011.

Shakira is one of the world's most powerful Latina celebrities. She was born Shakira Isabel Mebarak Ripoli in Colombia in 1977. Her father is Lebanese and her mother is Colombian. As a child, Shakira loved to dance. She also wrote song lyrics. By the time she was 10, she was singing and dancing in talent competitions. She began recording albums in 1990. She acted in a Latin TV show. In 1995, she recorded the album *Pies Descalzos* (Barefoot). It was a big success.

In 1998, she won two Latin Grammy awards. She began writing and recording songs in English. In 2001, her album *Laundry Service* sold more than 13 million copies. Shakira continued to record and perform her songs. She won more awards.

In 2003, Shakira become a Goodwill Ambassador for UNICEF. She travels around the world, raising awareness for children in need. She created the Pies Descalzos Foundation. There are six foundation schools in Colombia. Children who need help can attend. The schools give children a safe place to learn. Children are also given food. They can take art and music lessons. School workers even help their parents find work.

EDUCATING GIRLS

Shakira wants to help children around the world. As a Goodwill Ambassador for UNICEF, she has made visits to Bangladesh, Azerbaijan, and India. In India, she met with a group of poor girls who weren't even 14 years old. But they were already married. It's common in India for girls to marry very young. They can't choose their husbands. Most girls drop out of school when they marry. Shakira hopes to convince people that it's important to educate girls.

Shakira walks with children to celebrate the construction of a new school in Columbia funded by her Foundation.

6 Dorothy Dandridge: Best Actress Oscar Nominee

Dorothy Dandridge was an American actress, singer, and dancer at a time when African Americans were often treated unfairly. She was born in 1922 in Ohio. Her mother was an entertainer. Her father left before she was born. Dandridge sang and danced at church meetings in the South. She went to Hollywood in the 1930s. She got small parts in movies. She became a popular nightclub singer in New York and Las Vegas. At the time, African Americans weren't allowed to go everywhere whites could. Dandridge couldn't sit in the audience or swim in the pool of hotels where she sang.

In 1954, Dandridge got the lead role in an all-black film, *Carmen Jones*. It was rare then for films to have all-black casts. The story was a remake of an opera. It was a big success. Both black and white audiences liked it. The film was popular in Europe as well as the United States. Dandridge became well known. She was named one of the world's most beautiful women. She became the first African American nominee for Best Actress at the Academy Awards.

Dandridge's success in *Carmen Jones* did not pave the way for

Dandridge performing in the 1950s.

continued success. There weren't many starring roles for African American women at the time. Most roles were for small parts, such as a maid or someone's mother. Many people found romance between blacks and whites unacceptable. This made it hard for Dandridge to get work acting. When she died at the age of 42, she was deeply in debt.

$100,000

Amount Dorothy Dandridge was paid for her role in *Carmen Jones*.

- Racial discrimination kept Dandridge from succeeding.
- She was ranked the 5th most beautiful woman in the world.
- She could sing and act.

7

Julia Louis-Dreyfus: One of TV's Most Awarded Stars

Julia Louis-Dreyfus at the Emmys in 2017.

Julia Louis-Dreyfus is one of America's most successful sitcom stars. She was born in New York in 1961. Her mother was a tutor and writer. Her father was a wealthy businessman. Her parents split up when she was one year old. Louis-Dreyfus went to a private girls' school in Maryland. Then she studied acting at Northwestern University. She was active in a comedy troupe in Chicago. When a producer from the TV show *Saturday Night Live* (SNL) saw her, he offered her a job. At the age of 21, she left college and moved to New York.

After three years on SNL, Louis-Dreyfus left the show. She starred in sitcoms. She acted in movies. In 1989, she joined the sitcom *Seinfeld*. She played the main character's ex-girlfriend. The show ran from 1990–1998. Louis-Dreyfus won her first Emmy for that role. After *Seinfeld*, she starred in more sitcoms. She won more Emmys for her comedy acting. In 2010, she won a star on Hollywood's Walk of Fame. In her most recent sitcom, *Veep*, she won six Emmys in a row for lead actress in a comedy.

Louis-Dreyfus has donated money to Feeding America. This charity provides meals to children and families in need. She is also a champion of clean energy. Her house is made of reused wood and powered by solar energy. She drives an electric car. In 2017, Louis-Dreyfus found out she had breast cancer. She has since spoken out on the importance of health care for all people.

9

Number of Screen Actors Guild awards Julia Louis-Dreyfus has won

- Louis-Dreyfus also has a Golden Globe Award.
- She was the first actress to win Emmys for three different series.
- She shares the record with Cloris Leachman for most Emmys won by a single actor.

Louis-Dreyfus at the WorkHuman Conference in 2017 speaking about inclusion and culture in the workplace.

8

Dolly Parton: Promoting Education

Dolly Parton is a country music icon and actress. Her life has been called a "rags-to-rhinestones" story. She was born in Tennessee in 1946. She was one of 12 children. Her parents were poor farmers. The family lived in a one-room cabin in the woods.

Dolly loved music. She sang, wrote songs, and played guitar on local radio and TV shows when she was 10. When she finished high school, she went to Nashville to be a country singer.

A country music star named Porter Wagoner became Parton's mentor. Parton performed on his TV show. RCA Records recorded Parton and Wagoner. Their songs were very successful. Parton began to write pop music. Her pop songs were as successful as her country music. She also acted in several popular films, such as *Nine to Five* in 1980.

In 1986, Parton opened Dollywood. This is a theme park in Tennessee. It brings jobs and income to people in an area of poverty near where she grew up. In 1988, she started the Dollywood Foundation. This group helps promote education for children

Dolly Parton at the 50th Annual CMA Awards in 2016.

The Governor's Books from Birth Foundation distributes Imagination Library books free of charge to children up to the age of five.

in the area. She also started the Imagination Library in her hometown. The purpose is to help children learn to read and write. Books are mailed for free to families with preschool-age children.

THINK ABOUT IT

Dolly Parton was very poor as a child. She became very wealthy as an adult. Do you think her childhood influenced her decision to work for education? If yes, in what way?

1995

Year when Dolly Parton began Imagination Library

- Parton's father never learned to read or write.
- Parton wanted to help children love to read at a young age.
- The Imagination Library program has spread from Tennessee to countries around the world.

9

Rita Moreno: EGOT Winner

Rita Moreno with her Oscar in 1962.

1962

Year when Rita Moreno became the first Latina to win an Oscar

- Moreno is in her 80s and still working.
- President Barack Obama awarded her the National Medal of Arts in 2010.
- She is one of only 12 people to have won an EGOT.

Rita Moreno is a Puerto Rican actress, dancer, singer, and role model. She was born Rosita Dolores Alverio in 1931 in Puerto Rico. She grew up in New York City. Moreno took dance lessons. She dubbed voices for American children in Spanish versions of films. At age 13, she got a part in a Broadway play. At 18, she got a role in a film.

Moreno found more work in films. But she had trouble getting the parts she wanted. Filmmakers wanted to put her in ethnic roles. For example, in *The King and I*, she played an enslaved woman. In 1961, she had a part in *West Side Story*. It was a musical. She acted and danced. She won the Oscar for Best Supporting Actress. But she still had trouble getting mainstream roles.

From 1971–1977, Moreno starred in *The Electric Company*. This was a children's TV show. She won a Grammy for this in 1972. In 1975, she won a Tony for a part in a Broadway play. In 1977, she was on *The Muppet Show*. She won an Emmy for that role. This made her the second woman and third person to win an EGOT, which stands for Emmy, Grammy, Oscar, and Tony.

Moreno at the Grammy's in 2015.

LA PIONERA

Moreno didn't have any role models when she was growing up. There were no Puerto Rican film stars in the United States she could look up to. The Hispanic community calls her *La Pionera*. That means the pioneer. She became a role model for younger Latina actresses.

10

Meryl Streep: Most-Nominated Actress

Meryl Streep at a movie premier in New York.

Some critics say Meryl Streep is the best actress alive today. She was born Mary Louise Streep in 1949 in New Jersey. She started acting in high school. After college she moved to New York City. She began work as an actress. Her role in *The Deer Hunter*, a film about the Vietnam War, was widely praised. She went on to star in many successful films. She was able to play a wide range of roles. In 2003, Streep was nominated for the 13th time for an Academy Award. This broke the previous record of 12 nominations for Katharine Hepburn.

Streep acts in serious and funny roles. She plays likeable and unlikeable characters. She does voices in animated films. She speaks with different accents. Her face is very expressive.

Streep is also active in social causes. She and her husband,

Streep accepts the Presidential Medal of Freedom from President Barack Obama in 2014.

Don Gummer, started the Silver Mountain Foundation for the Arts. They give money to museums and theaters. They give money to help pay for programs for young artists and actors. They donate to education programs for low-income students. Streep also speaks out for women's rights. She wants equal pay for male and female actors. She funds a program to help women over age 40 succeed in the film industry.

THINK ABOUT IT

Streep accepted a Golden Globe Award in January 2018. In her speech, she spoke out about a political issue. Some fans praised her for this. Others criticized her. What do you think?

21

Number of Meryl Streep's Oscar nominations as of December 2018

- Streep has won Oscars for Best Actress and Best Supporting Actress.
- Streep has also been nominated for 31 Golden Globe awards.
- So far, she has won eight Golden Globes.

11

Ella Fitzgerald: The First Lady of Song

Ella Fitzgerald in 1946.

Ella Fitzgerald was an American jazz singer. She was born in Virginia in 1917. Her parents split up soon after. She and her mother moved to New York City. Fitzgerald loved to sing. She often went to Harlem to hear musicians perform at the Apollo Theater. When Fitzgerald was 15, her mother died. For a time, Fitzgerald was homeless.

In 1934, Fitzgerald entered a talent contest at the Apollo Theater. She sang her favorite jazz song. The audience loved her. Soon after, Fitzgerald met bandleader Chick Webb. He hired her to travel with his band. At the age of 21, she made a record that sold a million copies. Fitzgerald's career took off. It kept going for 60 years. She performed around the world. She worked with the big jazz musicians of the time. She was known for a special way of singing called scat. She used her

HARLEM

Harlem is a neighborhood in New York City. It is known as the home of the Harlem Renaissance. This was a time in the 1920s when African Americans created new forms of music, literature, dance, and art. The Apollo Theater is in Harlem. There are many soul food restaurants and art museums there as well.

voice to copy the sound of a horn. People called her the First Lady of Song.

Fitzgerald used her fame and fortune to help others. She donated money to help needy children. In 1993, she created the Ella Fitzgerald Foundation. It works to help kids at risk love reading and music. It provides health care, food, shelter, and counseling to people in need. It also pays for research to cure diabetes and heart disease.

$12.50

Ella Fitzgerald's weekly pay as a member of Chick Webb's band in 1935

- Fitzgerald was famous for her clear, joyful voice and wide vocal range.
- She won 14 Grammy awards.
- She starred in films and on TV.

Fitzgerald performs with Dizzy Gillespie, Ray Brown, Milt Jackson, and Timme Rosenkrantz in New York in 1947.

12

Tina Fey: Mark Twain Prize Winner

Tina Fey is an American comedy writer, actress, and producer. She was born Elizabeth Stamatina "Tina" Fey in 1970 in Pennsylvania. Her father was a university grant writer. Her mother worked at a financial institution. Fey and her brother did comedy acts together when they were kids. She studied drama at the University of Virginia. She then moved to Chicago, where she trained in comedy.

In 1997, Fey was hired as a writer for *Saturday Night Live* (SNL). After two years, she became head writer. It was the first time a woman had that job. In 2001, the SNL writers won an Emmy. In 2004, Fey started to write and star in films. *Mean Girls* was her first. Critics praised the film. It earned a lot of money.

Tina Fey in 2019.

In 2006, Fey wrote, produced, and starred in the TV series *30 Rock*. It ran for seven seasons. Fey won three Emmys in a row. In 2008, she also did skits on SNL. She played Sarah Palin, the Republican vice-presidential nominee. Fey's satire was very popular. Next, Fey created the comedy series *Unbreakable Kimmy Schmidt*. In 2010, Fey was given the Kennedy Center's Mark Twain Prize for American Humor.

Fey with her book *Bossypants.*

11

Tina Fey's age when she wrote a school book report on comedy

- As a child, Fey watched TV comedy shows with her parents.
- She wrote a satire column for her high school newspaper.
- She later wrote a book about her life called *Bossypants*.

THE MARK TWAIN PRIZE

Mark Twain was an American writer. He wrote *The Adventures of Tom Sawyer* and *The Adventures of Huckleberry Finn.* He lived from 1835–1910. His books were satire. He used humor to raise awareness about social issues such as racism. The Mark Twain Prize honors writers who use satire to raise awareness of social injustice.

Out of the Shadows

Pearlena Igbokwe

Universal Television hired Pearlena Igbokwe as their president in 2016. She is in charge of creative programming. She oversees comedies such as *SuperStore*. Before this job, she was a vice president at NBC Entertainment. She worked at Showtime for 20 years before that. Igbokwe was born in Nigeria.

Ava DuVernay

Ava DuVernay was the first African American to win a directing Oscar. She won for the film *Selma*. She is the highest paid African American woman director in American film history. She also directed *A Wrinkle in Time*. She won the 2012 Sundance Film Festival's Best Director Prize.

Ava DuVernay in 2015.

Sarah Barnett at the Emmys in 2017.

Sarah Barnett

Sarah Barnett was head of BBC America. In 2018, she was promoted to be in charge of four TV channels: AMC, Sundance TV, BBC America, and IFC. AMC became popular with shows like *Mad Men*, *Breaking Bad*, and *The Walking Dead*. Before BBC America, Barnett was at Sundance TV.

Victoria Alonso

Victoria Alonso is a vice president of production at Marvel Studios. She worked on *Black Panther*, *Avengers: Infinity War*, and *Guardians of the Galaxy Vol. 2*. In 2017, she was the first woman to win the Visual Effects Society (VES) Award. Alonso is praised for paving the way for women and Latinas in the film industry.

Glossary

activist
A person who fights for a social cause.

album
A collection of musical recordings.

civil rights
Basic personal rights such as life and liberty.

discrimination
The act of treating people unfairly because of their differences.

dub
To add in voice on a film in a different language.

ethnic
From a minority group.

genre
A category of music, such as pop or folk.

induct
To add someone to a group.

lyrics
The words of a song.

mainstream
Normal or conventional; the idea, attitude, or action of most of the people.

mentor
A wise adviser or teacher.

sitcom
Short for situation comedy, a type of TV show.

Read More

Halligan, Katherine. *HerStory: 50 Women and Girls Who Shook Up the World.* New York: Simon & Schuster, 2018.

Medina, Nico. *Who Was Aretha Franklin?* New York: Penguin, 2018.

Mullarkey, Lisa, and John Mullarkey. *Get Ella to the Apollo.* Minneapolis, MN: Calico, 2015.

Index

About the Author

Marne Ventura has written over 100 books for children. A former elementary school teacher, she holds a master's degree in education from the University of California. Marne and her husband live on the central coast of California.